HATHA YOGA

• MANUAL I •

by

Saṁskṛti *and* Veda

Published by

The Himalayan International Institute
of Yoga Science and Philosophy
Honesdale, Pennsylvania

ISBN 0-89389-016-2

Copyright 1977
Second Printing 1978
Second Edition 1979

HIMALAYAN INTERNATIONAL INSTITUTE
OF YOGA SCIENCE AND PHILOSOPHY
RD 1, Box 88, Honesdale, Pennsylvania 18431

Dedicated to our reverend teacher

Shri Swami Rama of the Himalayas

from whom we have been learning.

The authors would like to express a special thanks to the following people whose work was invaluable in bringing this book to print: Sri O. P. Tiwari, David Coulter, Ph.D., Mary Bergstedt, Theresa O'Brien and Janet Zima.

Table of Contents

I.   Introduction vi

II.   How to Use this Manual 1

III.   Attitudes, Hints, and Cautions 4

IV.   Yama and Niyama 6

V.   Diaphragmatic Breathing .8

VI.   Stretching Exercises 11

             Simple Standing Posture 12
             Horizontal Stretch 14
             Overhead Stretch 16
             Side Stretch 18
             Simple Back Stretch 20
             Angle Posture—*Konasana* 22
             Torso Twist 26
             Swimming Stretch 28
             Cat Stretch 30
             Butterfly 32
             Leg Cradles 34
             Symmetrical Stretch 38

VII.   Sun Salutation—*Soorya Namaskara* 41

VIII.   Asanas 59

             Easy Posture—*Sukhasana* 62
             Kneeling Posture—*Vajrasana* 63
             Crocodile—*Makarasana* 64
             Corpse—*Shavasana* 66
             Back Bending Posture—*Urdhvasana* 68
             Hand-to-Foot Posture—*Padahastasana* 70
             Triangle—*Trikonasana* 72
             Tree—*Vrikshasana* 74
             Cobra—*Bhujangasana* 78
             Half Boat—*Ardha-Naukasana* 80
             Boat—*Naukasana* 82
             Half Locust—*Ardha-Shalabhasana* 84
             Locust—*Shalabhasana* 85
             Half Bow—*Ardha-Dhanurasana* 86
             Bow—*Dhanurasana* 88
             Knees-to-Chest Posture 90

Wind Eliminating Posture—*Pavanamuktasana* 91
Single Leg Lifts—*Utthita Ekapadasana* 92
Double Leg Lifts—*Utthita Dwipadasana* 95
Balance on Hips—*Utthita Hasta-padasana* 96
Rocking Chair 98
Half Plow—*Ardha-Halasana* 100
Plow—*Halasana* 102
Inverted Action Posture—*Vipritakarani* 104
Shoulder Stand—*Sarvangasana* 106
Half Fish—*Ardha-Matsyasana* 108
Arch Posture 109
Twisting Posture 110
Half Spinal Twist—*Ardha-Matsyendrasana* 112
Churning—*Chalan* 114
Posterior Stretch—*Paschimottanasana* 116
Head-to-Knee—*Janushirasana* 118
Inclined Plane 120
Child's Posture—*Balasana* 122
Symbol of Yoga—*Yoga Mudra* 124
Squatting Posture 126
Cow's Face—*Gomukhasana* 128
Lion—*Simhasana* 132
Abdominal Lift—*Uddiyana Bandha* 134
Preparation for Head Stand 136
Head Stand—*Shirshasana* 138

IX.   Relaxation Exercise 142

X.   Channel Purification—*Nadi Shodhanam* 144

Index 147

ॐ सहनाववतु । सह नौ भुनक्तु ।
सह वीर्यं करवावहै । तेजस्वि नाव
धीतमस्तु । मा विद्विषावहै ।
ॐ शान्तिः ! शान्तिः !! शान्तिः !!!

PRAYER OF HARMONY
for Teacher and Student

OM Sahana Vavatu
Sahanau Bhunaktu
Sahaviryam Karavavahai
Tejasvinavadhitamastu
Ma Vidvishavahai
OM Shantih Shantih Shantih

Oh God, Protect us both together,
Accept us both together,
Let us achieve strength,
Let our learning ever shine,
Let us not resent each other.
OM Peace Peace Peace

Introduction

Yoga is one of the six schools of Indian philosophy. Unlike the other schools, it is accepted not only as a philosophy but also as a science and practical method of self-unfoldment, the application of which can lead to the absolute Truth. Because of this emphasis on practice rather than theory, the other schools of philosophy frequently refer to and utilize the experiences of the yogis, particularly their exploration of the conscious, unconscious and superconscious levels of their being.

In the history of Indian philosophy, yoga developed in many different aspects including: *karma yoga*—the yoga of action; *bhakti yoga*—the yoga of devotion; and *jnana yoga*—the yoga of knowledge. Besides the development of these different methods of spiritual practice, hatha yoga gained popularity among ascetics and those interested in the physiological conditions of the body and the control of breath. Because of its emphasis on *asanas* and *pranayama* rather than on philosophical matters, hatha yoga was not accepted as a formal school of philosophy.

Raja yoga, the royal path, which is correctly called *astanga yoga* or the eightfold path, includes the teachings of all paths of yoga. The practice and philosophy of raja yoga was codified by Patanjali, approximately 200 A.D., in his *Yoga Sutras*, a work consisting of 196 aphorisms or sutras. The eight *angas* or limbs of this path are:

External
1. *Yamas* — restraints
2. *Niyamas* — observances
3. *Asanas* — postures
4. *Pranayama* — control of breath
5. *Pratyahara* — control of senses

Internal
6. *Dharana* — concentration
7. *Dhyana* — meditation
8. *Samadhi* — Self-realization

Patanjali describes the *yamas, niyamas, asanas, pranayama* and *pratyahara* as external forms of practice and *dharana, dhyana* and *samadhi* as internal forms.

Patanjali's teaching of raja yoga begins with the five *yamas* and *niyamas*, the moral disciplines of yoga. These disciplines are as important for the beginning student as they are for the accomplished yogi.

In his *Yoga Sutras*, Patanjali accepts some principles of hatha yoga, but does not describe *asanas* or *pranayama* in detail. He emphasizes concentration and meditation, the *dharana* and *dhyana* aspects of raja yoga.

In the second chapter, sutra forty-six, Patanjali defines *asana* as "a particular posture of the body, which is steady and comfortable." In the system of raja yoga this definition applies to those postures which are used in the practice of meditation. This is made clear in sutra forty-seven: "The posture is perfected, made steady and comfortable through relaxing, not forcing the effort and by fixing the consciousness on the Infinite."

The hatha yoga school treats the subject of *asanas, pranayama*, and other more subtle forms of practice at great length. Its exponents developed these aspects of raja yoga after Patanjali's codification of the *Yoga Sutras*. Approximately 1350-1550 A.D. Swatmarama systematized and codified the science of hatha yoga in his extensive work, the *Hathayogapradipika*.

In this classical text on hatha yoga, Swatmarama explains that "ha" represents sun and "tha" represents moon. Hatha yoga means the practice of uniting *prana* and *apana*, sun and moon. "Ha" and "tha" are also symbolic expressions of *pingala* and *ida* (the two main channels of subtle energy in the body), of right and left, of male and female, of active and passive.

Swatmarama begins the *Hathayogapradipika* by explaining that hatha yoga is a stairway for those who wish to attain the lofty raja yoga. Thus, yoga should not be practiced for the sake of perfecting the postures only. This is a particular problem in the West where yoga has become especially popular in the form of hatha yoga. The goal of hatha yoga ultimately is to attain the goal of raja yoga.

There are from at least eighty-four to one hundred and eight *asanas*. As such, it is not always easy to discover which postures should be practiced by beginning students and which should be practiced by advanced students. In this book, the writers have included those *asanas* which are easy and beneficial for beginning students and have paid particular attention to the needs and abilities of Western students. If students follow the practices of this book as outlined they will be greatly aided in understanding the basic principles of hatha yoga.

Matthew Monsein, M.D.
April 15, 1978

How to Use This Manual

This manual is designed for students who have had no exposure to hatha yoga or who have recently begun to practice. Read the sections Attitudes, Hints, and Cautions, Yama and Niyama, and Diaphragmatic Breathing carefully before attempting any of the exercises or postures. Many of the postures have been simplified, but in such a way that the benefits have not been minimized. The preliminary steps shown are important in order to perfect the postures; master them before adding the advanced variations. If you have no serious physical problems, you can successfully learn most of the postures in three to four months of daily practice. It is important to read all the instructions, including the preliminary exercises, cautions, and benefits before attempting a posture. Remember that no manual on a practical subject, such as hatha yoga, can substitute for studying with a qualified teacher. If you are practicing on your own, exercise care and common sense at all times.

We recommend two supplimentary texts in conjunction with this manual. *Joints and Glands Exercises*, edited by R. M. Ballentine, M.D. and *Lectures on Yoga* by H. H. Swami Rama. The joints and glands and stretching exercises should be practiced for two to three weeks before beginning the postures. Older persons, or those who have not done physical exercises for some time should practice these for a longer period. *Lectures on Yoga* gives a philosophical overview of the system of raja yoga and discusses the *yamas* (first rung), *niyamas* (second rung) and *pranayama* (fourth rung) in greater detail, whereas the main focus of this manual is *asanas* (third rung).

Read the section on diaphragmatic breathing carefully before practicing the *asanas*. Spend a few minutes each day practicing diaphragmatic breathing until it becomes a natural function. In all the exercises and *asanas*, deep, even breathing is recommended. Beginners should not practice breath retention in any of the postures.

Every day practice a few stretching exercises, as well as the sun salutation, in

1

order to limber the body before beginning the *asanas*. If preparatory exercises are shown for an *asana*, practice these for one to two weeks before attempting the *asana* itself.

If you have recently undergone surgery, have any serious physical problem, or have a tendency toward high blood pressure (this latter case especially refers to the topsy-turvy postures), check with your physician before beginning the practice of *asanas*.

Begin with three repetitions of each posture. Slowly increase the duration of each posture and reduce the repetitions.

Balance is an important principle of hatha yoga. Backward bending postures should be balanced with forward bending postures. You can follow a forward bend with a backward bend (such as in the 2nd and 3rd positions of the sun salutation), or a number of backward bending *asanas* with a number of forward bending *asanas*. This basic principle of balance also applies to the repetitions of *asanas*. If you practice an exercise or *asana* three times on one side, practice it three times on the opposite side. However, if one side of the body is more stiff than the other, practice extra repetitions on that side until both are equally supple.

The postures are presented in an order which is a good general guide for practice. This is not meant as a hard and fast rule, but rather, as a guideline for slowly working from the active postures to those which move the body less. Begin with the stretches, the sun salutation, the abdominal lift, and the standing postures; follow with the backward bending postures on the stomach, which slowly and gently limber the spinal column for the more difficult *asanas*. In the backward bending postures there are two important points to remain aware of, the neck and the small of the back. The fish should always follow the shoulderstand and plow as it counter-balances the extreme forward bend in the neck from these two postures. Follow the shoulderstand-plow-fish series with the forward bending and sitting postures. Read with extra care the cautions and hints for the headstand before attempting this posture.

Relax in the postures, be aware of the breath and concentrate on the area of stretch. Move smoothly and gently going into, holding, and coming out of the postures. By keeping the breath even, smooth, and deep, each posture can be held with little or no movement. This is the first step in perfecting the *asanas* and in preparing to sit in a steady and comfortable posture for meditation.

Relaxation between the postures can be done in either the crocodile or corpse posture. The crocodile is used to relax between the postures lying on the stomach; the corpse, before and after postures, and also between the postures lying on the back.

If you experience difficulty doing a posture, first mentally envision yourself doing it, *then*, do it physically. If you can't do it mentally, *don't* do it physically.

All of the postures described in this manual, with the exception of the easy posture, *sukhasana*, are cultural postures, i. e., *asanas* for physical well-being. Practice *sukhasana* until you can sit with the body steady, erect, and comfortable for some time. Other meditative postures include: the lotus posture—*padmasana*, the accomplished posture—*siddhasana*, and the auspicious posture—*swastikasana*. Sitting postures such as the kneeling posture—*vajrasana*, are done only as preparation for one or more of the cultural postures.

Practice the channel purification exercise *(nadi shodhana)*, after the *asanas* and the complete relaxation exercise.

If there are times when you are unable to practice all of the postures, then choose one or two of each type. Be certain to include: the sun salutation, abdominal lift, cobra, plow-shoulderstand-fish series, a twisting posture, a forward bending posture and a balance posture.

Attitudes, Hints and Cautions

Asanas, unlike other physical disciplines, are not correctly practiced unless the proper mental attitudes are cultivated; they should be practiced with patience, determination, and joy. A number of preparations are helpful in bringing about the proper mood.

• Set a specific time each day for your practice. This should be a time when you do not feel pressured into rushing through the postures. Pick a time when the likelihood of disturbances is at a minimum. It is also important to practice your postures every day, regularly. In this way you will find yourself unconsciously preparing for the postures before actually beginning them.

• The most beneficial times to practice *asanas* are the mornings and evenings. Practicing *asanas* in the morning helps you remain calm and alert the entire day. In the evening, *asanas* relieve the day's tensions and help you to later enjoy an undisturbed and peaceful sleep. In the morning the body is stiffer, so take greater care practicing your *asanas*. A warm bath or shower when you first get up will help relax your muscles. Then, before beginning the *asanas*, practice sufficient stretching and limbering exercises. You should save the more difficult *asanas* for the evening.

• Practice your *asanas* in a clean, quiet, well-ventilated area, one which is free from drafts. Wear loose and comfortable clothing; cotton or other natural materials are best, for they allow the body to breathe. It may also be helpful to have an 'asana suit' or set of clothing which you use exclusively for your practice.

• Always practice postures on an empty stomach. Wait at least four hours after a heavy meal and two hours after a light meal. Do not drink liquids immediately before doing postures. As we state in the introduction to the *asanas*, many of the postures increase intra-abdominal pressure and affect the internal organs. Practicing with food in the stomach will cause discomfort and can lead to more serious problems. For this same reason we also recommend that the bowels and bladder be empty.

• Women should not practice *asanas* during menstruation. This is a natural cleansing time in which many physical and physiological changes occur so you should allow your body to rest. Practicing *asanas* may cause cramps and excess bleeding. Also, during pregnancy you should check with your physician before continuing any of the exercises or *asanas*.

• Do not become discouraged if your body does not respond in the same way each day. Sometimes you will discover that the posture you found easy yesterday is not so easy today. It takes time and regular practice for both the body and mind to stabilize. The important thing is to keep practicing regularly. Approach each day's practice as an opportunity to study anew the body's movements and capacities. Never develop a sense of competition either with fellow students or with oneself. This reduces your practice of *asanas* to a level of mere physical performance.

• Study your body and its movements. Be aware of your capacity and learn not to go beyond it. In any posture, concentrate the mind on the muscles that are being stretched and learn to distinguish between stretching and straining. Any shaking, straining, or pain indicates that either you are doing something incorrectly or that you have gone beyond your capacity. Gentleness and regularity in practice is far superior to forcing the body into a posture prematurely. Let common sense prevail.

• Let the body movements flow evenly and gently with the breath. Generally, whenever you expand the chest you will inhale naturally; whenever you bend the torso toward the lower half of the body you will exhale. Breathe evenly and deeply without jerks and pauses. The breath, however, should not become a source of distraction through over-conscientiousness, it should be allowed to flow easily and naturally. In almost all of the postures, we have recommended even, deep breathing. Breath retention is not recommended for beginners.

• Follow any exertion by relaxation. The length of relaxation depends on each individual; your breathing and heartbeat should return to normal before doing the next posture. However, never allow the mind to drift toward sleep either between postures or during the relaxation exercise at the end of your postures.

Yama and Niyama

The *yamas* and *niyamas*, the first two rungs of *astanga* yoga, make up the gateway through which we must pass if we are to enter the path of yoga. They are the moral foundation upon which the successful practice of yoga is built, and should be practiced to perfection on all levels—thought, word and action. We are not, however, expected to master these principles completely before beginning the practice of *asanas, pranayama,* and the other rungs of yoga. The *yamas* and *niyamas* are ideals whose perfection we will become aware of on increasingly subtler levels as we progress on the path of yoga. It is necessary that the increased awareness and self-control obtained in the preliminary practice of yoga be used in a positive and constructive manner, as it is only those of pure mind and heart who can attain the highest states of their being.

The *yamas* are moral disciplines and restraints which regulate our relationships with other individuals. The *niyamas* are constructive observances designed to organize our personal daily lives. Briefly, the *yamas* and *niyamas* include:

YAMA

AHIMSA   Non-violence with mind, action, and speech, non-hurting, non-injuring, non-harming, and not killing.

SATYA   Truthfulness. This refers to the avoidance of all falsehood, exaggeration and pretense and is necessary for the unfoldment of our intuitive, discriminating faculties.

ASTEYA   Non-stealing. This refers not only to stealing physical objects but also to taking credit for anything that is not rightly ours.

BRAHMACHARYA   Literally, "walking in *Brahman.*" *Bramacharya* is the control of sensual desires, allowing one to use that energy for higher purposes.

6

Brahmacharya is frequently translated as celibacy, however, it more properly refers to continence, in either celibate or married life.

APARIGRAHA   Non-possessiveness. This refers to using the things of the world for their intended purposes, without a feeling that you own them or that you are owned by them.

NIYAMA

SHAUCHA Purity. Purify the body by eating pure, healthy foods and by practicing cleansing exercises. Purify the mind by ridding oneself of undesirable thoughts and emotions.

SAMTOSHA   Contentment. You should not allow outside influences to disturb your inner tranquility.

TAPAS   Literally, "that which generates heat." This refers to those actions, disciplines, and austerities which purify the mind and the body and increase man's desire for enlightenment.

SVADHYAYA   Self-study. This refers to the study of the scriptures and of the internal states of consciousness.

ISHWARA PRANIDHANA   Literally means "surrender to the Ultimate." When you unite your individual will with that of a higher principle, all egotism, pettiness, and selfishness are removed.

Diaphragmatic Breathing

Although breathing is one of man's most vital functions, it is little understood and often done improperly. Most people breathe shallowly and haphazardly, going against the natural rhythmic movement of the body's respiratory system. Diaphragmatic breathing, on the other hand, promotes a natural, even breath movement which strengthens the nervous system and relaxes the body. The importance of deep, even breathing in practicing the *asanas* cannot be over-emphasized.

Respiration is normally of two types, costal and abdominal. According to Dr. Catherine P. Anthony in her *Textbook of Anatomy and Physiology*, costal or shallow breathing is characterized by "an outward, upward movement of the chest due to contraction of the external intercostals and other chest elevating muscles." Abdominal or deep breathing is characterized by "an upward, outward movement of the abdominal wall due to the contraction and descent of the diaphragm." This latter method of breathing is practiced during the *asanas*.

The principle muscle of abdominal breathing is the diaphragm, a strong, horizontal, dome-shaped muscle. It divides the thoracic cavity which contains the heart and lungs from the abdominal cavity which contains the organs of digestion, reproduction, and excretion. The other major muscles important in deep breathing are the *rectus abdominis*, the two strong vertical muscles of the abdomen. These muscles work in co-operation with the diaphragm.

During inhalation the diaphragm contracts and flattens; it pushes downward, causing the abdominal muscles to relax and slightly extend. In this position the lungs expand, creating a partial vacuum which draws air into the chest cavity. During exhalation the diaphragm relaxes and returns to its dome-shaped position. During this upward movement the abdominal muscles contract and carbon dioxide is forced from the lungs.

Diaphragmatic breathing has three important effects on the body:

1)   In diaphragmatic breathing, unlike shallow breathing, the lungs fill

completely, providing the body with sufficient oxygen.

2)   Diaphragmatic breathing forces the waste product of the respiratory process, carbon dioxide, from the lungs. When breathing shallowly some carbon dioxide may remain trapped in the lungs causing fatigue and nervousness.

3)   The up and down motion of the diaphragm gently massages the abdominal organs; this increases circulation to these organs and thus aids in their functioning.

In diaphragmatic breathing you use a minimum amount of effort to receive a maximum amount of air; as such, it is our most efficient method of breathing.

Technique:

Lie on the back with the feet a comfortable distance apart; gently close the eyes and place the hands on the abdomen in order to feel the movement of the abdominal muscles.

Inhale and exhale through the nostrils slowly, smoothly, and deeply. There should be no noise, jerks, or pauses in the breath. Exaggerating the normal breathing process, consciously pull in the abdominal muscles while exhaling. Students who find difficulty in practicing this diaphragmatic movement may want to use their hands to gently push the abdominal muscles in when exhaling. When inhaling be aware of the abdominal wall pushing out. There should be little or no movement of the chest.

Practice this method of deep breathing 3 to 5 minutes daily until you clearly understand the movement of the diaphragm and the abdominal muscles. The body is designed to breathe diaphragmatically; gradually it should again become a natural function.

STRETCHING EXERCISES

SIMPLE STANDING POSTURE

Stand firmly with the feet 6 to 12 inches apart. Keep the head, neck, and trunk in a straight line and relax the arms and hands at the sides of the body. Breathe evenly.

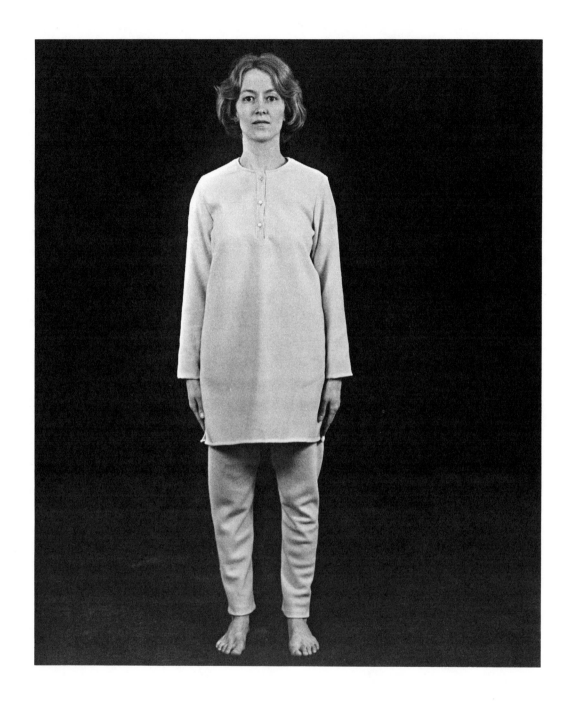

SIMPLE STANDING POSTURE

HORIZONTAL STRETCH

Horizontal Stretch

Assume the simple standing posture.

Inhale and slowly raise the arms to shoulder level with the palms facing downward. Breathe evenly.

Imagine that the body has a line dividing it down the center. Stretch progressively from the chest, to the shoulders, the upper arms, the elbows, the lower arms, the wrists, the hands, the fingers, and the finger tips. Stretch as far as possible.

Keeping the arms in the same position slowly relax from the finger tips to the chest.

Exhale and slowly lower the arms and return to the simple standing posture. Concentrate on the breath until the body relaxes completely.

Repeat this exercise three times.

HORIZONTAL STRETCH

OVERHEAD STRETCH

FIRST POSITION

Assume the simple standing posture.

Begin inhaling and slowly raise the arms out to the side with the palms facing downward. When the arms reach shoulder level slowly turn the palms upward. Continue inhaling and raise the arms above the head; place them shoulder width apart with the palms facing each other. (This basic method of raising the arms overhead will be used when practicing the other stretching exercises, unless otherwise stated.) Breathe evenly for three complete breaths.

Keeping the feet firmly on the floor stretch the body upward. Stretch progressively from the lower legs, to the upper legs, the abdomen, the stomach, the chest, the shoulders, the upper arms, the lower arms, the hands, the fingers, and the finger tips.

Keeping the arms overhead, slowly relax downward from the finger tips to the feet. Exhale and slowly lower the arms. At shoulder level turn the palms downward and slowly return to the simple standing posture. Concentrate on the breath until the body relaxes completely.

Repeat this exercise three times.

SECOND POSITION

Raise the arms as described above for the overhead stretch, but this time, after raising the arms, place the palms together in the prayer position and place the upper arms next to the ears.

Progressively stretch and relax the body as described in the overhead stretch.

Repeat this exercise three times.

OVERHEAD STRETCH
FIRST POSITION

SIDE STRETCH

Assume the simple standing posture.

Begin inhaling and slowly raise the right arm out to the side with the palm facing downward. When the arm reaches shoulder level turn the palm upward. Continue inhaling and raise the arm until it is next to the ear.

Keeping the feet firmly on the floor, stretch the entire right side of the body upward. Do not allow the body to bend forward or backward or the right arm to bend.

Begin exhaling and slowly bend at the waist, sliding the left hand down the left leg. Breathe evenly for three complete breaths.

Inhaling, slowly bring the body back to an upright position.

Exhaling, slowly lower the arm to shoulder level, turn the palm downward, and return to the simple standing posture. Concentrate on the breath until the body relaxes completely.

Repeat the side stretch in the opposite direction.

NOTE: For a more intense stretch repeat this posture with the legs together.

SIDE STRETCH

SIMPLE BACK STRETCH

FIRST POSITION

Assume the simple standing posture.

With the fingers facing downward, place the heels of the hands on either side of the spine just above the buttocks.

Exhaling, gently push the hips forward, slowly letting the head, neck, and trunk bend backward as far as possible without straining.

Inhaling, return to the standing pose, keeping the hands in the same position.

SECOND POSITION

Place the hands on either side of the spine directly below the rib cage. Repeat the stretch as described in the first position.

THIRD POSITION

Place the hands on either side of the spine directly below the shoulder blades. Repeat the stretch as described in the first position.

Keeping the entire body relaxed, slowly bend the body forward as far as possible. Hold this position until all the muscles of the back relax completely.

NOTE: This forward bend balances the effects of the backward bending postures.

SIMPLE BACK STRETCH

21

ANGLE POSTURE · *Konāsana*

FIRST POSITION

Assume the simple standing posture with the feet two to three feet apart.

Placing the arms behind the back, grasp the right wrist with the left hand. Keep the heels in line and place the right foot at a 90° angle from the left.*

Inhaling, turn the body toward the right foot.

Exhaling, bend forward from the hips and bring the head as close to the knee as possible. Breathe evenly; hold this position for five counts.

Inhaling, slowly raise the body, exhaling, turn to the front. Turn the right foot so that it faces forward.

Repeat the exercise on the left side.

* Beginning students may turn the left foot slightly inward (to the right) if it is more comfortable.

SECOND POSITION (Arm Variation)

Keeping the arms straight, interlace the fingers behind the back. With the right foot at a 90° angle from the left, turn the body and bend forward from the hips, bringing the head toward the knee. Raise the hands overhead as far as possible. Breathe evenly; hold this position for five counts.

Inhaling, slowly raise the body and turn to the front.

Repeat the exercise on the left side.

Repeat the exercise to the front, with both feet facing forward.

ANGLE POSTURE–*KONASANA*

THIRD POSITION (Hand Variation)

With the arms straight, interlace the fingers behind the back and press the palms together.

Exhaling, raise the arms and bend forward as far as possible. Breathe evenly and hold for five counts.

Inhaling, push the hands toward the floor and bend the head, neck, and trunk back as far as possible without straining. Breathe evenly; hold for five counts.

Slowly return to a standing position and relax.

ANGLE POSTURE—*KONASANA*
THIRD POSITION

TORSO TWIST

FIRST POSITION

Assume the simple standing posture with the feet two to three feet apart.

Raise the arms overhead; interlace the fingers. Keeping the arms next to the ears and stretching the body from the rib cage upward, rotate the upper torso, arms, and hands in a clockwise direction.

Inhale as the body leans to the right and to the back; exhale as the body leans to the left and to the front.

Repeat three times clockwise and then three times counterclockwise. Continue by moving into the second position.

NOTE: In this position the waist, hips and legs remain stationary.

SECOND POSITION

Keeping the hips stationary and bending from the waist, repeat the above exercise three times clockwise and three times counterclockwise. Continue by moving into the third position.

THIRD POSITION

Keeping the legs stationary and bending from the hips as far as possible, rotate and twist the entire upper part of the body in a large circle. Repeat three times clockwise and three times counterclockwise.

Relax. Concentrate on the breath.

TORSO TWIST

27

SWIMMING STRETCH

Assume the simple standing posture with the feet three feet apart.

Raise the arms overhead and face the palms forward.

Exhaling, slowly start lowering the trunk toward the right foot. Move the arms and shoulders imitating a swimming motion, alternately stretching first one side of the body and then the other. Bring the head toward the knee and the hands toward the foot as far as possible.

Inhaling, and continuing the same swimming motion, slowly return to a standing posture.

Repeat, lowering the trunk toward the left leg; slowly return to standing.

Repeat lowering the trunk straight forward; return to standing.

Relax.

SWIMMING STRETCH

CAT STRETCH

FIRST POSITION

(a) Kneel on all fours with the arms straight and the back parallel to the floor.

(b) Begin exhaling, arch the back, pull the buttocks in, and bring the head toward the chest. Hold this position without inhaling for three seconds.

(c) Begin inhaling, bend the back, expand the chest, and raise the head as far as possible.

Hold this position without exhaling for three seconds.

Relax; then repeat three times.

SECOND POSITION

Kneel on all fours as in the first position.

(d) Exhaling, bend the right knee, slowly lower the head and bring the knee to the forehead. Hold this position without inhaling for three seconds.

(e) Inhaling, extend the leg, expand the chest and raise the head as far back as possible. Feel the stretch along the leg, back and neck. Hold this position without exhaling for three seconds.

Repeat this exercise three times.

Repeat three times with the left leg.

Once the first and second positions can be done comfortably, practice positions (a) through (e) in a series. Repeat three times.

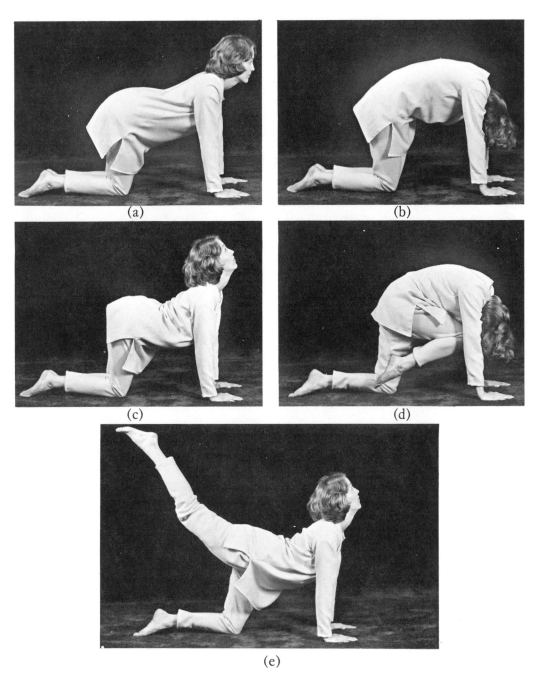

(a)

(b)

(c)

(d)

(e)

CAT STRETCH

BUTTERFLY

FIRST POSITION

Bend the legs at the knees, place the soles of the feet together and bring the heels as close to the body as possible. Interlace the fingers and place them around the toes; rest the elbows on the upper thighs.

Slowly and gently bounce the legs; try to lower the knees toward the floor. It is important to keep the movement of the legs gentle and relaxed. Do not try to force the knees to the floor.

Exhaling, bend forward trying to touch the head to the toes. Hold this position for three complete breaths.

Inhaling, slowly raise the trunk.

Release the hands and extend the legs. Alternately, gently lower and raise the knees with a bouncing motion in order to relax the muscles of the inner thighs.

SECOND POSITION

Arm variation in the forward bend: place the elbows as close to the knees as possible, rest the hands on top of the feet, aligning the fingers with the toes.

BUTTERFLY

LEG CRADLES

FIRST POSITION

Sit cross-legged.

Cradle the right leg, holding the knee with the right hand and holding the foot with the left. Gently rock the leg from side to side, moving it from the hip.

Repeat with the left leg.

LEG CRADLES
FIRST POSITION

35

SECOND POSITION

Cradle the right leg, by placing the foot in the bend of the left elbow and the knee in the bend of the right elbow. Interlace the fingers in front of the leg.

Gently rock the leg from side to side, gradually pulling it higher and closer to the body. Hold both the knee and the foot to the chest for five counts.

Relax and repeat with the left leg.

LEG CRADLES
SECOND POSITION

SYMMETRICAL STRETCH

Lie on the floor; place the feet together with the toes and heels touching. With arms overhead and the palms together, stretch the torso in an upward direction and the legs in a downward direction, keeping the body symmetrical.

Breathe evenly and hold this position for ten seconds.

NOTE: In this posture the emphasis is on stretching and aligning the vertebrae. It may also be done in a standing position.

SYMMETRICAL STRETCH

SUN
SALUTATION

SUN SALUTATION·*Soorya Namaskāra*

The sun salutation is a series of twelve positions, each flowing into the next, in one graceful, continuous movement. These exercises are performed a few times before beginning the *asanas*. While facing the rising sun with an attitude of worship, the names of twelve seed mantras are silently repeated in accordance with each movement. The sun shines for all and excludes none from its light and life-giving energy. In performing salutations to the sun, we ask that light and energy to unfold within us.

Although not considered part of traditional yoga postures by many schools of hatha yoga, *soorya namaskara* is an excellent warm-up exercise; it stretches and limbers the spine and limbs. While performing *soorya namaskara*, coordinate the twelve positions with the breath; inhale as you go into one position and exhale as you go into the next. Retain the breath only in the fifth position.

At first, practice the entire exercise three times; practice it slowly without going beyond your capacity. During the first week become familiar with the movements only. It is important that from position 3 through 10 the hands remain in the same place. Once the positions are familiar you can coordinate the breathing and body movements. The sun salutation sets the proper mood of inner and outer harmony essential to the true practice and goal of hatha yoga.

Relax the body completely before beginning your yoga *asanas*.

Benefits: While asleep, the body lies in an inactive condition. During this time, the conscious mind ceases to function, the metabolic rate decreases, circulation of the body fluids slows and the functional capacity of the rest of the body reduces considerably. Upon awakening, the body and mind must make a transition from this inactive condition to one of activity. *Soorya namaskara* aids in this transition by massaging and stimulating the glands, organs, muscles and nerves of the body. The breath rate increases, bringing more oxygen into the lungs, thus quickening the heart rate. This in turn causes more blood to pass through the lungs, picking up oxygen, and therefore, sending a greater supply of oxygenated blood throughout the different parts of the body.

The movements in the sun salutation incorporate five *asanas*. These include: position 2 (*urdhvasana*), position 3 (*padhastasana*), position 5 (*padangushthasana*), position 7 (*bhujangasana*) and position 8 (*dandasana*). However, their benefits are not as great as when performed for longer periods of time.

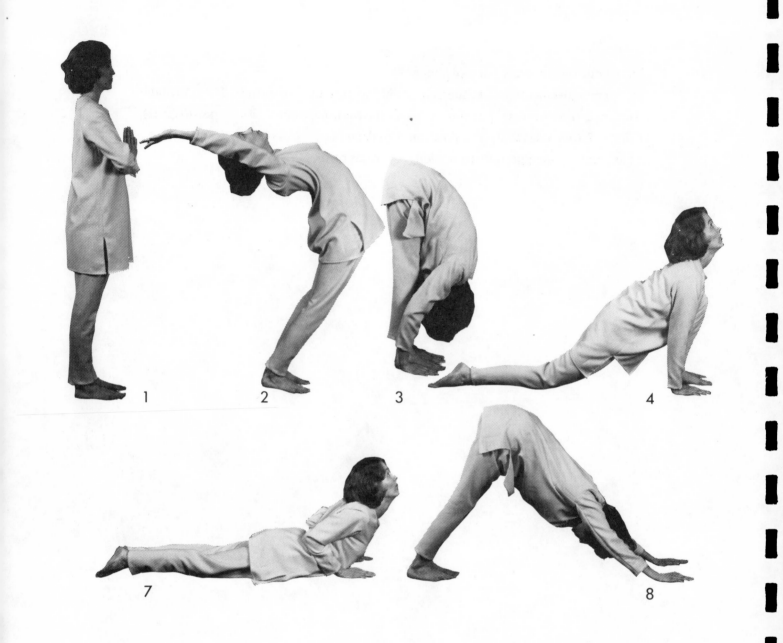

WITH HANDS IN PRAYER I FACE THE SUN, FEELING LOVE AND JOY IN MY

BEFORE THE SUN'S RADIANCE AND PLACE MY FACE TO THE GROUND IN

TO ACHIEVE SUCH HEIGHTS, I MUST BE AS THE DUST OF THE EARTH.   I

AND AGAIN SURRENDER.   I STAND TALL AS I REMEMBER THE TRUE SUN

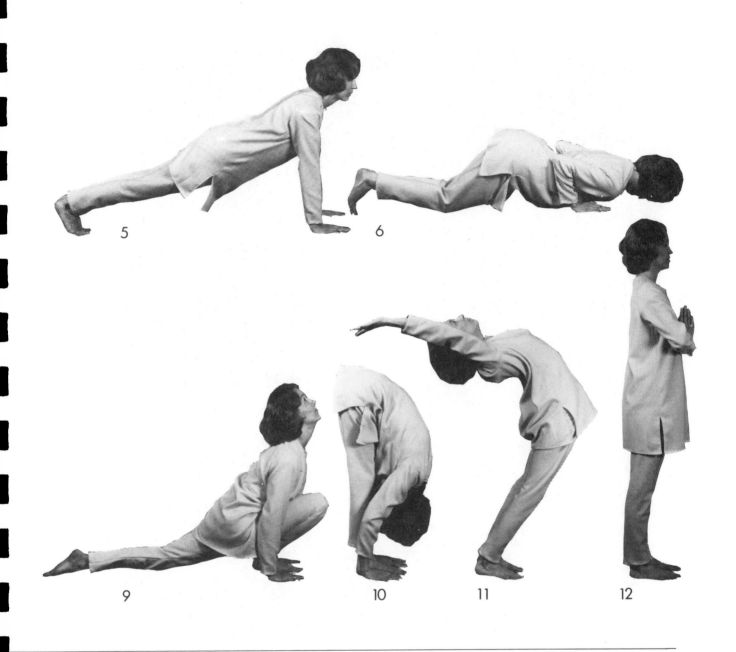

HEART.   I REACH OUT AND LET THE SUN FILL ME WITH WARMTH. I BOW

HUMBLE RESPECT.   I LIFT MY FACE TO THE SUN AND THEN REMEMBER,

STRETCH UP TOWARDS ITS LIGHT TRYING TO REACH THE GREATEST HEIGHTS

IS WITHIN ME.

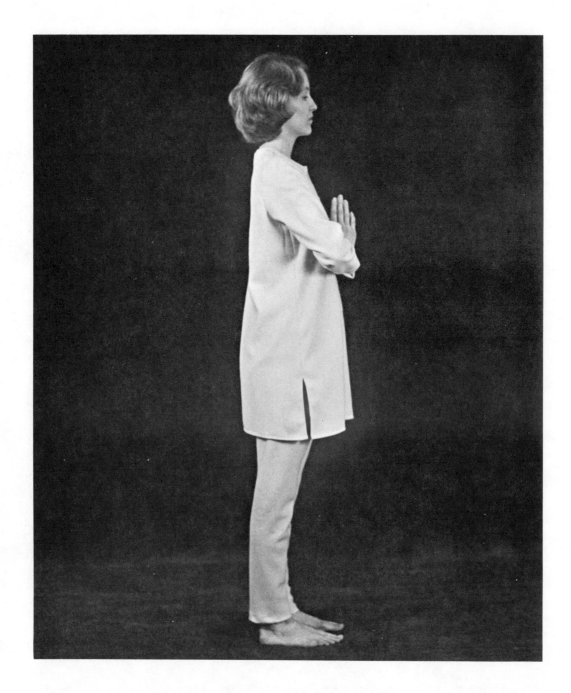

POSITION 1: Exhale

Stand firmly with the head, neck, and trunk in a straight line. Beginners can stand with the feet slightly apart. With palms together in prayer position, place the hands before the heart and gently close the eyes. Standing silently, concentrate on the breath and mentally repeat a short positive affirmation.

POSITION 2: Inhale

Inhaling, slightly lower and stretch the hands and arms forward with the palms facing downward. Raise the arms overhead until they are next to the ears. Keeping the legs straight, and the head between the arms, arch the spine and bend backward as far as possible without straining.

POSITION 3: Exhale

Exhaling, bend forward from the hips, keeping the back straight and the arms next
to the ears. Continue bending; place the palms next to the feet, aligning the fingers
with the toes. Bring the head to the knees keeping the legs straight.
NOTE: If you can not place the hands on the floor without bending the legs, then
lower only as far as possible without straining.

POSITION 4: Inhale

In this position bend the knees if necessary in order to place the hands on the floor. Inhaling, stretch the right leg back, rest the right knee and the top of the right foot on the floor, and extend the toes. The left foot remains between the hands; the hands remain firmly on the floor. Arch the back, look up, and stretch the head back as far as possible. The line from the head to the tip of the right foot should form a smooth and graceful curve.

49

POSITION 5: Retain

Retain the breath. (This is the only position in which the breath is held.) Curl the toes of the right foot, extend the left leg, placing it next to the right. The arms remain straight and the body forms an inclined plane from the head to the feet. This position resembles a starting push-up position.

POSITION 6: Exhale

Exhaling, drop first the knees and then the chest to the floor, keeping the tips of the fingers in line with the breasts. Tuck in the chin and place the forehead on the floor.

In this position only the toes, knees, hands, chest, and forehead touch the floor. The nose does not touch the floor and the elbows remain close to the body.

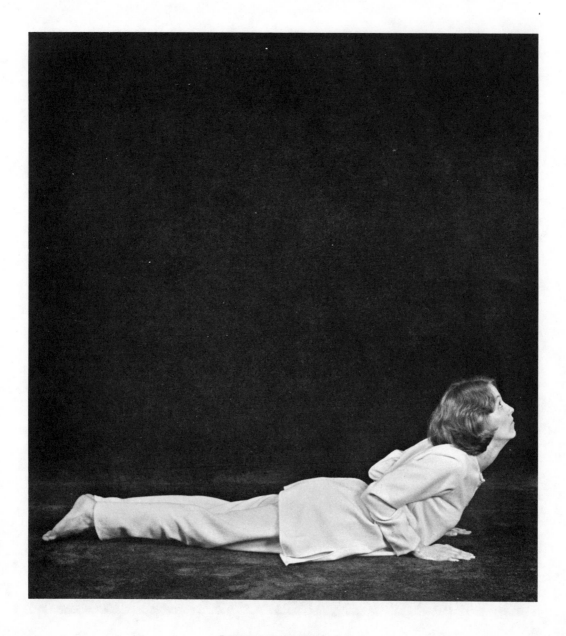

POSITION 7: Inhale

Without moving the hands and forehead, relax the legs and extend the feet so that the body rests flat on the floor. Inhaling, slowly raise the head. First, touch the nose and then the chin to the floor; then, stretch the head forward and upward. Without using the strength of the arms or hands, slowly raise the shoulders and chest; look up and bend back as far as possible.

In this posture the navel remains on the floor. To lift the thorax, use the muscles of the back only. Do not use the arms and hands to push the body off the floor, but to balance the body. Keep the feet and legs together and relaxed.

POSITION 8: Exhale

Without repositioning the feet and hands, straighten the feet so that they point toward the hands. Exhaling, straighten the arms and push the buttocks high in the air. Bring the head between the arms and try to press the heels to the floor.

POSITION 9: Inhale

Inhaling, bend the right knee and place the right foot between the hands. Align the toes with the fingers. Rest the left knee and the top of the foot on the floor and extend the toes. Arch the back, look up, and bend back as far as possible.

POSITION 10: Exhale

Exhaling, place the left foot beside the right keeping the palms on the floor. Straighten the legs and bring the head to the knees.

POSITION 11: Inhale

Inhaling, slowly raise the body, stretching the arms out, up, and back. Remember to keep the arms next to the ears and to keep the legs straight.

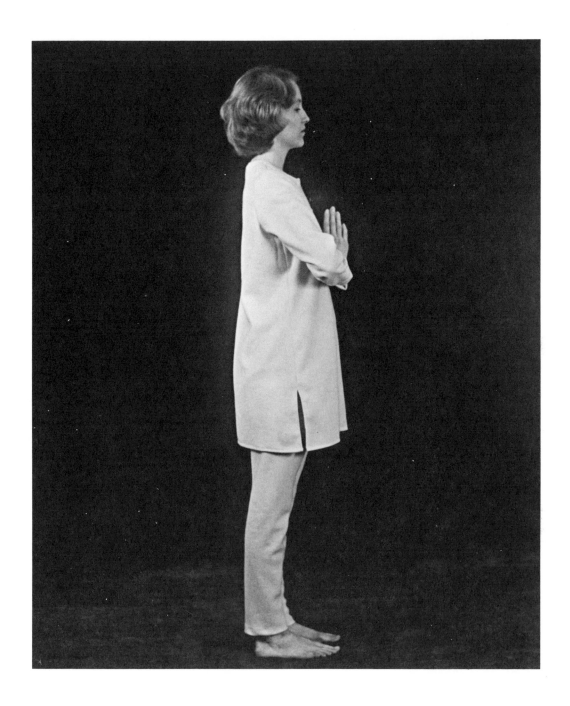

POSITION 12: Exhale

Exhaling, return to an erect standing position. Slowly lower the arms and bring the hands to the chest in prayer position.

Repeat the sun salutation, but alternate the leg movements by extending the opposite leg in positions 4 and 9.

ASANAS

Asanas

"Asanas make one firm, free from maladies, and light of limb."

Hathayogapradipika of Svatmarama, Chapter 1, verse 17

This statement summarizes concisely the benefits and purpose of *asanas*.

First, to prepare the body for meditation, making it calm, steady and firm;
Second, to free the body from disease (dis-ease), to develop superb health
    so the mind is not distracted by aches and pains after the body has
    been made steady for meditation; and
Third, to bring lightness to the body, not only literally, by reducing excess
    weight and increasing suppleness, but also figuratively, counteracting
    heaviness and depression by developing lightness of feeling and ex-
    pression.

The benefits of the postures are primarily on the vertebral column and internal organs. Almost every posture either involves back bending in one direction or another, or involves carefully focusing the mind on maintaining a perfect posture. In addition to the direct effects of developing a healthy spine, the bending and twisting postures also have important effects on the internal organs. For example, many of them cause an increase in intra-abdominal pressure, which in turn forces stagnant venous blood out of the organs, thereby encouraging their perfusion with arterial blood. These postures also supplement the constant movement and gentle massaging of the viscera (the internal organs) that occurs with diaphragmatic breathing.

The topsy-turvy postures have important effects on both circulation and respiration. A large pool of venous blood in the legs normally depends on muscular activity for being "pumped" past valves and back to the heart, activity that is sadly lacking in many people in our society. The upside-down postures quickly drain this blood from the legs and improve circulation. The diaphragm is our most

60

important muscle of respiration, but is frequently misused and almost universally underused. You can quickly learn diaphragmatic breathing in a mild upside-down posture, such as the inverted action posture, because the weight of the abdominal organs pushes the diaphragm to an especially high position in the chest during exhalation. You can relate to this visually by observing the resulting cavitation on the front side of the abdomen. During inhalation, the diaphragm must then push the abdominal organs up against the force of gravity and this in turn pushes out the abdominal wall, again providing visual feedback that is easily observable.

All of the postures help prepare you for meditation. Sitting in a comfortable and easy posture with the head, neck, and trunk straight is a serious problem for beginning students. Many years of bad habits, influences and attitudes have encouraged us to develop poor posture. This can result in physical ailments such as low back pain, easy fatigue and incorrect and shallow breathing. Systematically practicing the various postures and breathing exercises in this manual will greatly aid you in strengthening the muscles of the back, stretching and limbering the other muscles and ligaments of the body, and improving flexibility of the joints, thereby preparing you for the practice of meditation.

Benefits are also listed for many of the individual postures. These comments are the culmination of thousands of years of self-observation by teachers and students who have devoted their lives to understanding the working of the human body. Full appreciation and understanding of the effects of the postures can never be achieved unless the postures are practiced. Your own body is the finest laboratory facility imaginable, and nothing can substitute for the direct personal knowledge that is the primary tradition of this science.

EASY POSTURE·*Sukhāsana*

This is a simple cross-legged posture.

Sit with the head, neck, and trunk straight. Place the left foot beneath the right knee and the right foot beneath the left knee. Each knee rests on the opposite foot.

This posture is useful for beginners and older people, especially if the other postures are painful or uncomfortable.

KNEELING POSTURE·*Vajrāsana*

Sit in a kneeling position with the head, neck, and trunk straight. Place the hands, palms downward, above the knees.

This sitting posture (also called the Zen posture) is used in two *asanas* described in this manual, the yoga mudra and the lion. It is also useful in developing an awareness of good posture.

CAUTION: Increase the time in this posture very slowly. Injury to the peroneal nerve of the lower leg which can cause permanent dropping of the foot, may result from staying in the posture too long.

CROCODILE·*Makarāsana*

Lie on stomach, placing the legs a comfortable distance apart and pointing the toes outward. Fold the arms in front of the body, resting the hands on the biceps. Position the arms so that the chest does not touch the floor.

Concentrate on the breath and observe the effects of diaphragmatic breathing. While inhaling, feel the abdominal muscles gently press against the floor; while exhaling, feel the chest raise slightly. Let the body relax completely.

NOTE: If you find it uncomfortable to point the feet outward you may turn them inward.

Benefits:
- Excellent for relaxation, particularly before and between the prone back-bending postures.

- This position not only necessitates diaphragmatic breathing, but it also teaches you how it feels to breathe diaphragmatically. When you inhale you feel the abdomen press against the floor; when you exhale you feel the abdominal muscles relax. Diaphragmatic breathing causes this same abdominal movement in all positions; however, while lying in the crocodile posture, it cannot go unnoticed.

CROCODILE—*MAKARASANA*

CORPSE·*Shavāsana*

Lie on the back and gently close the eyes. Place the feet a comfortable distance apart, place the arms along the sides of the body, with the palms upward and the fingers gently curled. The legs should not touch each other, nor should the arms and hands touch the body. Do not lie haphazardly or place the limbs far apart, but lie in a symmetrical position.

In this *asana* the body resembles a corpse; it lies still and relaxed. It is important to refrain from drowsing; keep the mind alert and focused on the flow of the breath.

Between *asanas* remain in this posture only until respiration and heartbeat return to normal. For relaxation before and after the sequence of *asanas*, beginners should not remain in this posture for more than ten minutes.

Benefits:

- Between postures, it helps you to relax and to prepare the mind for the next posture in sequence.

- Before postures, it centers the mind and prepares it for focusing on the *asanas*. It helps you to relax the skeletal muscles, enabling you to go further into the postures while reducing the likelihood of injuries.

- After postures, it reduces all traces of fatigue.

- At midday, as a break from your work, it relaxes and rejuvenates the mind and body.

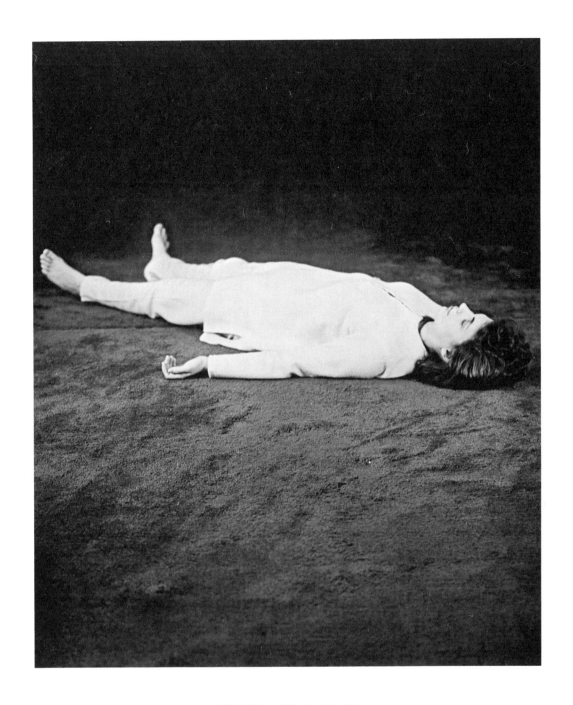

CORPSE–*SHAVASANA*

BACK BENDING POSTURE·*Urdhvāsana*

Stand firmly with the head, neck, and trunk in a straight line, feet together.

Inhaling, stretch the hands and arms overhead until they are next to the ears. Keeping the legs straight, and the head between the arms, arch the spine and bend backward as far as possible without straining. Breathe evenly; hold for two to five seconds.

Exhaling, lower the arms. Relax.

Benefits:

- Unlike the cobra, locust, and bow, this backbending posture uses gravity to help you go into the posture, allowing you to concentrate particularly on relaxation and on gently moving to the limit of the spine's flexibility.

BACK BENDING POSTURE—*URDHVASANA*

HAND~TO~FOOT POSTURE·*Pādahastāsana*

Stand with the head, neck, and trunk in a straight line, feet together.

Inhaling, stretch the hands and arms overhead until they are next to the ears.

Exhaling, bend forward from the hips, keeping the back straight and the arms next to the ears; grasp the toes with the fingers. Bring the head to the knees keeping the legs straight. Breathe evenly; hold for five to ten seconds.

Inhaling, raise the torso. Relax.

Benefits:

- Same benefits as in the sitting forward bend, however it is often more useful for beginners, since gravity aids one in moving to one's limit in the posture

- Relieves constipation

- Decreases excess abdominal fat

- Makes the spine supple and stretches the hamstring muscles

HAND-TO-FOOT POSTURE--*PADAHASTASANA*

TRIANGLE·*Trikonāsana*

VARIATION 1

Assume the simple standing posture with the feet three feet apart.

Inhaling, slowly raise the arms to shoulder level with the palms facing downward.

Twist the trunk to the right. Exhaling, bring the left hand to the inside of the right foot, keeping the arms and the legs straight. The arms remain in line with each other, and the right arm extends straight up. Look up and back at the right hand.

Breathe evenly; hold for five seconds.

Inhaling, slowly return to a standing position.

Repeat, bringing the right hand to the inside of the left foot.

Repeat on each side a total of three times.

VARIATION 2

Repeat the posture as described above turning the foot at a 90° angle. Place the hand on the floor at the inside of the foot.

NOTE: If you find it difficult in the beginning to place your hands on the floor, bend forward only as far as you can comfortably. The arms and legs should remain straight at all times. A simpler version of the triangle can be done by following the directions of the side stretch (see stretching exercises) with the feet two to three feet apart.

Benefits:

- Increases flexibility of the spinal column and hip joints

- Lengthens the hamstring muscles on the back of the thigh

TRIANGLE—*TRIKONASANA*

TREE·*Vrikshāsana*

FIRST POSITION

Stand erect with the legs together.

Bend the right leg at the knee and slide the right foot up the left leg. Without bending forward, grasp the right ankle with the right hand and position the heel snugly against the perineum (the area between the genitals and the anus). Rest the bottom of the foot on the inside of the left thigh.

Balance steadily on the left foot. While inhaling bring the hands to the chest in a prayer position. Breathe evenly and hold for 15 to 20 seconds. Then relax by standing on both feet.

Repeat standing on the left leg.

In this posture the body remains balanced and still. You will find it helpful to fix your gaze on a stationary point a few feet away.

TREE—*VRIKSHASANA*

75

SECOND POSITION

When you feel steady and confident in the first position raise both arms overhead. Place the palms together, keep the upper arms next to the ears, and stretch the arms upward. Hold for 15 to 20 seconds.

THIRD POSITION

Instead of placing the foot as high on the leg as possible, place it on top of the thigh in the half lotus position. Bring the hands to the chest in a prayer position. Hold for 15 to 20 seconds.

FOURTH POSITION

Repeat the third position stretching the arms overhead and placing the palms together. Hold for 15 to 20 seconds.

Benefits:

- The development of poise and concentration which is helpful for the performance of all postures

TREE—*VRIKSHASANA*
FOURTH POSITION

COBRA·*Bhujaṅgāsana*

Lie on the stomach, with the forehead against the floor, and the body fully extended and relaxed. Bend the elbows, keeping them close to the body, and place the hands beside the chest. Place the palms down and align the finger tips with the nipples.

Inhaling, slowly raise the head. First, touch the nose and then the chin to the floor; then, stretch the head forward and upward. Without using the strength of the arms or hands, slowly raise the shoulders and chest; look up and bend back as far as possible. Breathe evenly; hold for five seconds.

Exhaling, slowly lower the body until the forehead rests on the floor. Relax. Repeat three times.

In this posture the navel remains on the floor. To lift the thorax use the muscles of the back only. Do not use the arms and hands to push the body off the floor, but to balance the body. Keep the feet and legs together and relaxed.

NOTE: There are many variations of this posture. One common variation entails using the arms to raise the thorax. We do not recommend this variation for beginners as it makes it easy for one to force the body beyond its capacity.

Benefits:

- Strengthens the muscles of the shoulders, neck and back

- Develops flexibility of the cervical vertebrae

- Corrects deviations of the spine

- Improves circulation to the intervertebral discs

- Expands the chest and develops elasticity of the lungs

- Is said to help low back pain, constipation, gastric pains, gas pains, backaches

COBRA--*BHUJANGASANA*

HALF BOAT·*Ardha-Naukāsana*

Lie on the stomach, place the forehead on the floor, and extend the arms straight overhead with the palms resting on the floor. Keep the feet and legs together and relaxed.

Inhaling, raise the chest, arms, and head from the floor while keeping the head between the arms. Breathe evenly; hold for five seconds.

Exhaling, lower the body. Relax.

Repeat three times.

NOTE: Both exercises of the half boat should be practiced for at least one week before attempting the boat pose.

HALF BOAT—*ARDHA-NAUKASANA*

Lie in the position described in the first half boat exercise. Keep the hands, arms, and chest relaxed; keep the legs straight and feet approximately 12 to 18 inches apart.

Inhaling, raise the legs and feet from the floor. Breathe evenly; hold for five seconds.

Exhaling, lower the legs. Relax.

Repeat three times.

BOAT·*Naukāsana*

The boat posture combines the two preparatory exercises shown. Assume the position described at the start of both exercises with the feet approximately 18 inches apart. Inhaling, simultaneously raise the arms and the legs until only the stomach remains on the floor. The body forms a gentle curve from the tip of the toes to the fingers. Breathe evenly; hold for five seconds.

Exhaling, lower the body. Relax.

Repeat three times.

NOTE: For a greater stretch, with the head between the arms try to look up at the ceiling. As the body becomes stronger the legs can be brought close together.

Benefits:

● Strengthens all the muscles of the back

● Increases intra-abdominal pressure and promotes better circulation to the internal organs.

BOAT—*NAUKASANA*

HALF LOCUST·*Ardha-Shalabhāsana*

Lie on the stomach, and place the chin on the floor. Keeping the legs together, point the toes outward, make fists, and extend the arms along the sides of the body.

Inhaling, raise the right leg as high as possible. The left leg remains relaxed; do not allow the knee to press against the floor, nor the body to twist sideways.

Breathe evenly; hold for ten seconds.

Exhaling, slowly lower the leg.

Repeat with the left leg. Alternately repeat the exercise three times with each leg.

NOTE: Practice the half locust for at least two weeks before attempting the full locust.

LOCUST·*Shalabhāsana*

Assume the position described at the start of the half locust. Place the fists under the top of the thighs, keeping the arms straight.

Inhaling, raise both legs as high as possible. Breathe evenly; hold for ten seconds.

Exhaling, slowly lower the legs.

Repeat three times. Then relax completely.

For beginning students the fists should remain under the thighs. This enables one to raise the legs and feet higher in the air. As the abdominal muscles and the muscles of the back become stronger the fists can be placed at the sides of the body.

Benefits:
- Strengthens the muscles of the lower back, thus improving sitting postures for meditation

- Reduces lower back pain tendencies.

HALF BOW · *Ardha-Dhanurāsana*

FIRST POSITION

Lie on the stomach, place the chin on the floor, and extend the right arm beside the body. Bend the left arm at the elbow and place it on the floor in front of the head. Bend the right leg at the knee, and with the right hand grasp the outside of the ankle.

Inhaling, raise the head, shoulders and chest; pull the leg up as far as possible without straining the muscles of the back. Breathe evenly; hold for five seconds.

Exhaling, slowly lower the leg and then the rest of the body.

Relax.

Repeat the exercise on the left side.

Alternating, repeat the exercise three times with each leg.

HALF BOW—*ARDHA-DHANURASANA*

SECOND POSITION

Lie in the position described at the start of the previous exercise.

Bend the right leg at the knee. This time grasp the inside of the right ankle with the left hand.

Inhaling, raise the head, shoulders, and chest, pulling the leg up as far as possible.

Exhaling, slowly lower the leg and then the rest of the body.

Relax.

Repeat the exercise on the left side.

Alternating, repeat the exercise three times with each leg.

BOW · *Dhanurāsana*

Lie in the position described at the start of the half bow.

Bend both legs at the knees. Keeping the arms on the outside of the legs, grasp the ankles.

Inhaling, raise the head, shoulders, and chest; then pull the legs up as high as possible. The body should resemble the smooth curve of a bow. Breathe evenly; hold for five seconds.

Exhaling, slowly lower the legs until the knees are on the floor, then lower the torso. Relax.

Repeat the exercise three times.

NOTE: Beginners should allow the legs to be apart.

Benefits:
- Develops flexibility of the spine.

- Stretches the abdominal muscles and massages them.

- Prepares you for more difficult backbending postures such as the wheel and the scorpion.

- Reduces fat

- Strengthens the knee joints

BOW—*DHANURASANA*

KNEES-TO-CHEST POSTURE

Lie on the back. Bend the legs at the knees and bring them to the chest. Wrap the arms around the legs, pulling them closer toward the chest. The head remains on the floor.

This posture is excellent for relieving strain in the lower back, particularly from the backward bending and inverted postures. You should hold the posture until this tension is released. Experiment in the posture by gently rocking back and forth or from side to side; hold the posture to one side and then to the other or simply hold the posture as described above. Discover which position best releases tension at any given time.

FIRST POSITION

WIND ELIMINATING POSTURE
Pavanamuktāsana

FIRST POSITION

Lie on the back. Exhaling, bend the right knee, wrap the arms around the leg and pull it toward the chest. Raise the head and bring the forehead toward the knee. Breathe evenly; hold for three to five seconds.

Exhaling, relax the body.

Repeat with the left leg.

SECOND POSITION

Repeat with both legs.

Benefits:

● Relieves gas in the lower digestive tract.

SINGLE LEG LIFTS·*Utthita Ekapādāsana*

Lie on the back, place the legs together, the arms along the sides of the body, and the palms on the floor.

Inhaling, slowly raise the right leg as high as possible. Keep both legs straight.

Breathe evenly; hold for five seconds. Exhaling, slowly lower the leg.

Repeat with the left leg. Alternating, repeat the exercise three times with each leg.

NOTE: Throughout the exercise, keep the shoulders, arms, and hands relaxed. While lifting the leg, do not press the arms against the floor, nor twist the body to the side. While raising one leg keep the opposite leg straight, resting it firmly on the floor. If beginning students find the single and double leg lifts difficult, practice for two to three weeks without concentrating on the breath. Once the abdominal and lower back muscles are strengthened, continue to practice the breathing as outlined.

VARIATION 1

Repeat the exercise as described above raising the leg only four inches from the floor.

VARIATION 2

Repeat the exercise as described above raising the leg at a 45° angle from the floor.

VARIATION 3

After raising the leg perpendicular to the floor, point the toe toward the ceiling and hold for three seconds. Then, push the heel toward the ceiling and again hold for three seconds. Relax the foot and slowly lower the leg. Alternating, repeat three times with each leg.

SINGLE LEG LIFTS—*UTTHITA EKAPADASANA*

VARIATION 4

After raising the leg, grasp the calf or, if possible, the ankle. Pull the leg toward your head; raising the shoulders from the floor try to touch the head to the knee. Breathe evenly; hold for three seconds.

Exhaling, relax and slowly lower the leg. Repeat with the other leg.

DOUBLE LEG LIFTS·*Utthita Dwipādāsana*

Inhaling, raise both legs until they are perpendicular to the floor. Breathe evenly; hold for five seconds.

Exhaling, slowly lower the legs.

VARIATION:

Repeat with both legs the variations of the single leg lifts.

95

BALANCE ON HIPS

Utthita Hasta-pādāsana

Lie on the back with the legs together and the arms beside the body. Stretching the hands toward the toes and keeping the arms and legs straight, raise both the trunk and the legs until only the hips remain on the floor. Hold for five seconds. Relax.

The balance on hips posture is sometimes referred to as the boat posture.

Benefits:
- Excellent for developing balance and strengthening the abdominal muscles

BALANCE ON HIPS—*UTTHITA HASTA-PADASANA*

ROCKING CHAIR

Preparatory Exercise for Plow

In a sitting position, bend the knees, bringing them up to the chest, and cross the legs at the ankles. With the arms on the outside of the legs, grasp the toes.

Keeping the head between the legs, rock backward as if in a backward somersault, and touch the toes to the floor behind the head. Now, rock forward in the same way, until the forehead touches the floor between the knees.

Using momentum to rock back and forth, repeat the exercise five times. In this exercise do not hold either the forward or the backward position. The emphasis is on limbering the vertebrae and stretching the muscles of the back.

ROCKING CHAIR

HALF PLOW·*Ardha~Halāsana*

Lie on the back, place the arms along the sides of the body and the legs together.

Inhaling, slowly raise both legs until they are perpendicular to the floor. Then, raise the hips off the floor, keeping the legs straight and together. Extend the feet beyond the head until the legs are parallel to the floor. Breathe evenly; hold for 10 to 15 seconds.

Exhaling, slowly lower the hips and return the legs to a perpendicular position. Continue exhaling and slowly lower the legs to the floor.

HALF PLOW—*ARDHA-HALASANA*

PLOW·*Halāsana*

Follow the instructions of the half plow but continue to lower the feet until the toes touch the floor behind the head.

Breathe evenly; hold for 15 to 20 seconds. Come out of this posture as described in the half plow pose.

Slowly increase your capacity until you can hold the plow comfortably for one minute.

Benefits:

- Lengthens the muscles of the back of the thighs and prepares the body for forward bending and sitting postures.

- Relaxes the muscles of the back and gently stretches the ligaments of the spinal column

- One of the most reviving and rejuvenating of all postures

- Massages, tones, and stimulates all internal organs, especially the intestines, spleen, and liver

- Beneficial for constipation

PLOW—*HALASANA*

INVERTED ACTION POSTURE

Viprītakarani

Assume the half plow pose. Place the hands on the hips on either side of the spine; place the elbows shoulder width apart.

Inhaling, raise both legs until they are perpendicular to the floor.

Breathe evenly, hold for 20 to 30 seconds.

Exhaling, slowly lower the hips and return the legs to a perpendicular position. Continue exhaling and slowly lower the legs to the floor.

Slowly increase your capacity until you can hold this posture comfortably for one minute.

Benefits:

● Blood drains from the legs into the body cavities, relieving varicose veins

● Diaphragmatic breathing can be learned effectively in this posture, due to the weight of the abdominal organs on the diaphragm (see introductory comments on benefits, p. 8).

INVERTED ACTION POSTURE—*VIPRITAKARANI*

SHOULDER STAND · *Sarvāngāsana*

Assume the inverted action posture.

Move the hands until the palms are as close to the shoulders as possible, with the fingers pointing toward the small of the back and the elbows firmly on the floor. Press the breastbone against the chin, gently at first and more firmly with experience. Keep the legs straight, relaxed, and perpendicular to the floor. Breathe evenly; hold for 20 to 30 seconds.

Slowly increase your capacity until you can hold this posture comfortably for one minute.

Benefits:
- As implied in the literal translation of *sarvagasana*, "all members posture," this posture benefits all parts of the body, the shoulders, arms, legs, head, neck, back and internal organs.
- Strengthens arms, chest, and shoulders
- Slims legs and hips
- Strengthens back and abdominal muscles
- Places gentle traction on the cervical vertebrae, keeping this important area healthy and flexible
- Venous drainage of the legs occurs quickly and completely, especially benefitting those with varicose veins
- As in the inverted action posture, diaphragmatic breathing is easily observed and learned
- Causes higher blood pressure and simple mechanical pressure in the neck which are said to rejuvenate the thyroid and parathyroid glands, making them function optimally. These important glands regulate body weight and metabolism by natural mechanisms.
- Reduces the occurrence of acute and chronic throat ailments
- Increases blood supply to all the important structures of the neck
- Considered by hatha yoga literature to be the "Queen of Asanas," and a panacea for internal organ ailments, especially those of old age. The shoulderstand combats indigestion, constipation, degeneration of endocrine glands, problems occurring in the liver, the gall bladder, the kidney, the pancreas, the spleen, and the digestive system.

SHOULDERSTAND—*SARVANGASANA*

HALF FISH·*Ardha~Matsyāsana*

Sit with the head, neck, and trunk straight, legs extended in front of the body. Lean back and place the elbows and forearms on the floor behind the body. Arch the back, expanding the chest and stretch the neck backward, placing the crown of the head on the floor. Pull the head closely towards the back.

Breathe evenly; hold for 15 to 30 seconds.

Gently lower the body to a prone position.

If it is more comfortable this posture can also be done from a prone position by arching the back and bringing the top of the head to the floor.

Benefits:
> Provides a stretch to the cervical vertebrae which complements that of the shoulderstand. It amplifies the effects of the shoulderstand and eliminates the slight stiffness in the neck and back which results from doing the shoulderstand alone.

> The chest is thrown out, promoting deep inhalation, giving good ventilation to the top of the lungs, and increasing their capacity.

ARCH POSTURE

Preparation for the Bridge

Lie on the back and place the arms along the sides of the body with the palms downward. Bend the knees and bring the heels next to the buttocks.

Inhaling, raise the chest, stomach, and hips off the floor as high as possible, keeping the arms and hands on the floor and the legs together.

Breathe evenly; hold for 5 seconds.

Exhaling, slowly lower the body. Relax. Repeat three times.

NOTE: When using this exercise to relax the back after the shoulderstand, beginners may support the back with the hands.

TWISTING POSTURE

Preparatory Exercise for the Spinal Twist

Lie on the back with the legs together and the arms extended from the shoulders.

Inhaling, bend the knees and draw them to the chest.

Exhaling, slowly bring the knees to the floor near the right elbow and at the same time twist the head to the left. Keep the shoulders firmly on the floor.

Breathe evenly; hold five seconds.

Inhaling, bring the knees back to the chest and the head back to the center.

Exhaling, repeat as described above, bringing the knees to the left elbow and turning the head to the right.

Alternating, repeat the exercise three times on each side.

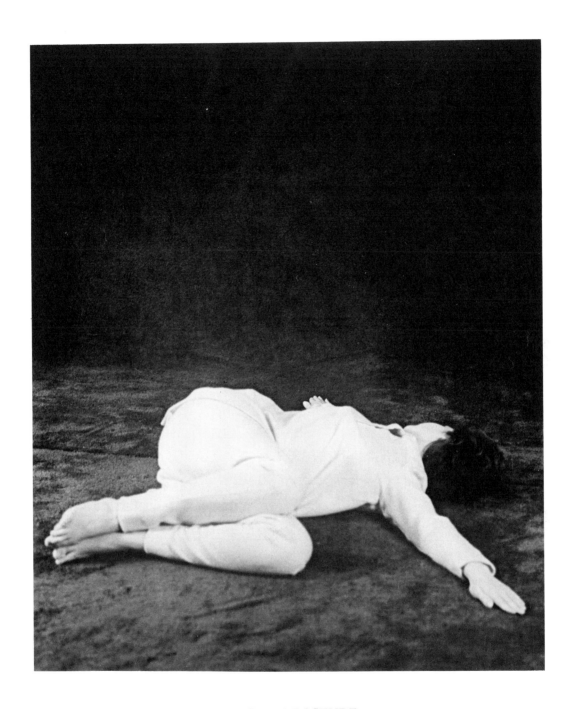

TWISTING POSTURE

HALF SPINAL TWIST

Ardha-Matsyendrāsana

Sit with the head, neck, and trunk straight. Extend the legs in front of the body.

Bend the right leg and place the right foot on the floor at the outside of the left knee.   Twist the body toward the right and place the right hand approximately 4 to 6 inches behind the right hip, fingers pointing away from the body. Bring the left arm over the outside of the right leg grasping the right foot with the left hand.

When bringing the arm over the leg you may bend slightly forward if necessary, however, do not arch back and then twist the body.

Keeping the back straight, twist the entire body to the right, looking over the right shoulder. Do not use the arms to force the body further into the twist, but use the arms for balance only.

Breathe evenly; hold five seconds.

Repeat on the opposite side. Alternating, repeat three times on each side.

Benefits:

> Provides a twist to the spinal column, stretching and lengthening the muscles and ligaments and keeping the spine elastic and healthy

> Alternately compresses each half of the abdominal region, squeezing those internal organs and promoting better circulation through them

> Combats constipation, reduces fat and improves digestion

HALF SPINAL TWIST—*ARDHA-MATSYENDRASANA*

CHURNING · *Chālan*

FIRST POSITION

Sit on the floor with the head, neck, and trunk straight; extend the legs in front of the body, keeping the legs as far apart as possible. Breathe evenly.

Bend forward and stretch the right hand toward the left foot. Keeping the left arm straight bring it behind the back. Bring the head toward the knee and look back toward the left hand.

Repeat the exercise on the opposite side.

Repeat the exercise ten times rhythmically moving from side to side.

SECOND POSITION — Preparation for Posterior Stretch

Sit with the legs together, extended in front of the body. Repeat as described above.

To increase the stretch on the forward bends, touch the floor on the outside of the foot rather than the toes.

THIRD POSITION — Preparation for Head-to-Knee Pose

Sit as described in Position 2. Bend the right leg at the knee and place the bottom of the foot on the inside of the left thigh. Position the heel snugly against the perineum. Repeat as described above.

CHURNING—*CHALAN*

Preparatory Exercise for Posterior Stretch

Sit with the head, neck, and trunk straight; extend the legs in front of the body.

Inhaling, raise the arms overhead. Exhaling, with the back straight and the head between the arms, bend forward as far as possible placing the hands comfortably on the legs. Breathe evenly; hold for five to ten seconds. Be sure that the backs of the knees remain on the floor.

Inhaling, slowly return to a sitting position. Repeat three times.

VARIATION

Spread the legs as wide apart as possible. Repeat the exercise as described above bending toward the right leg and holding the position.

Repeat the same on the left side.

Repeat bending straight forward.

POSTERIOR STRETCH
Paschimottānāsana

Follow the instructions as described in the preliminary exercise for the posterior stretch.

Grasp your two big toes with your thumbs and index fingers. Bring the head to the knees and place the elbows on the floor next to the knees. Breathe evenly; hold five to ten seconds.

Inhaling, return to a sitting position. Relax.

Benefits:
- Stimulates peristaltic movement of materials through the digestive tract and prevents constipation
- Stimulates entire abdominal area: kidneys, liver, stomach, spleen and pancreas
- Cures indigestion, poor appetite
- Is said to improve diabetic cases
- Stretches the hamstring muscles of the thigh and muscles and ligaments of the back, preparing the student for the sitting postures of meditation
- Gently massages the intervertebral disks, aids in their circulation, and develops flexibility of the spinal column

116

POSTERIOR STRETCH–*PASCHIMOTTANASANA*

Preparatory Exercise for the Head-to-Knee Posture

Sit with the legs extended. Bend the right leg at the knee and place the bottom of the foot on the inside of the left thigh. Position the heel snugly against the perineum. Repeat as described in the preparatory exercise for posterior stretch.

HEAD~TO~KNEE·*Janushirāsana*

Follow the instructions as described in the preliminary exercise for the head-to-knee posture.

Grasp the big toe of the extended leg. Bring the head to the knee and place the elbows on either side of the knee. Breathe evenly; hold five to ten seconds.

Inhaling, return to a sitting position.

Repeat on the opposite side. Relax.

Benefits:
- Useful for treating disorders of the prostate gland

- Helpful for men in controlling sexual urges because of the gentle pressure on the prostate gland

HEAD-TO-KNEE POSTURE—*JANUSHIRASANA*

INCLINED PLANE

Sit on the floor with the head, neck, and trunk straight. Keeping the legs together, extend them in front of the body. Leaning back slightly, place the hands on the floor eight to ten inches behind the hips, pointing the fingers away from the body.

Inhaling, raise the entire body until it forms an inclined plane from the shoulders to the toes. The bottom of the feet press against the floor, the arms remain straight, and the head drops back as far as possible.

Breathe evenly; hold five seconds.

Exhaling, slowly lower the body and return to a sitting position.

Repeat three times.

Benefits:
- Exercises the back muscles

- Complements the stretch of the forward bending postures

- Firms hips, abdomen, thighs, and arms

INCLINED PLANE

CHILD'S POSTURE·*Bālāsana*

Sit in a kneeling position with the top of the feet on the floor and the buttocks resting on the heels. Keep the head, neck, and trunk straight. Relax the arms and rest the hands on the floor, with the palms upward and fingers pointing behind you.

Exhaling, slowly bend forward from the hips until the stomach and chest rest on the thighs and the forehead touches the floor in front of the knees. As the body bends forward slide the hands back into a comfortable position.

NOTE: In the child's posture the body is completely relaxed and very compact. Do not lift the thighs or buttocks off of the legs. Keep the arms close to the body. If you experience discomfort, extend the arms above the head a shoulder width apart. Keep the arms straight and place the palms on the floor. Do not hold this posture for more than five minutes as it reduces the circulation in the legs.

Benefits:
- Relieves pain in the lower back from minor injury to muscles and ligaments

- Relaxes the back and promotes healing of more serious injuries, taking pressure off the intervertebral disks by providing a mild and natural form of traction

- Relieves strain in the lower back, particularly from forward bending postures

CHILD'S POSTURE—*BALASANA*

SYMBOL OF YOGA: *Yoga Mudrā*

Assume the easy sitting posture. Reach behind the back and grasp the right wrist with the left hand.

Exhaling, bend forward, keeping the back straight; slowly lower the body until the forehead rests on the floor in front of the legs. Keep the arms and hands relaxed and do not lift the buttocks off the floor.

Breathe evenly; hold 15 to 20 seconds.

Inhaling, slowly return to a sitting position, keeping the back straight. Release the hands, stretch the legs, and relax completely.

NOTE: This is a simplified version; in the full yoga mudra the student sits in the full lotus posture.

VARIATION:

Sitting in the kneeling posture, *vajrasana*, place the fists on the abdomen at the inside of the hip bones, bend forward, and place the forehead on the floor.

Breathe evenly; hold 15 to 20 seconds.

SYMBOL OF YOGA—*YOGA MUDRA*

SQUATTING POSTURE

Sit in a squatting position with the feet flat on the floor, eight to twelve inches apart.

Place the elbows on the knees, covering the face gently with the palms of the hands. Do not cover the nostrils or put pressure on the eyes.

Breathe evenly. Hold two to five minutes.

Benefits:
- This relaxation posture is especially useful for relieving dizziness and stomach cramps

- Helps in elimination; the thighs press against the abdomen creating pressure against the colon which in turn stimulates the bowel function

- Develops balance

- Stretches the muscles on the front side of the thigh

- Stimulates the peristaltic movement of materials through the digestive tract

- Relieves aching of the ankles and the knees

SQUATTING POSTURE

COW'S FACE·*Gomukhāsana*

FIRST STEP

Sit with the head, neck, and trunk straight.

Bend the left leg and place the heel next to the right hip.

Bend the right knee, crossing the leg over the left and place the heel next to the left hip. The knees are aligned and the buttocks remain firmly on the floor. Place the hands on the soles of the feet.

This posture is frequently referred to as the heroic posture (*veerasana*). The hands may be placed in a number of positions including: 1) the left hand on the right knee with the right hand on top, or 2) the fingers interlaced with the palms resting on the right knee or between the knees.

NOTE: Place the left leg on top if this is more comfortable.

COW'S FACE—*GOMUKHASANA*
FIRST STEP

129

SECOND STEP

Raise the right arm overhead, bending it at the elbow, and place the right palm between the shoulder blades. Lower the left arm behind the back, bending it at the elbow, with the palm facing outward. Clasp the fingers of both hands together. The right elbow points toward the ceiling and the left elbow toward the floor.

Breathe evenly; hold 15 seconds, stretching the arms, shoulders, and chest. Reverse the position of the hands and repeat.

NOTE: If you cannot clasp your hands, you may grasp a handkerchief or a cloth between them, using the cloth to slowly bring your hands together.

Benefits:
- Is said to remove rheumatism in the legs and cure hemorrhoids

- Especially good for learning to breathe diaphragmatically, since the relative immobilization of the thorax and shoulders makes thoracic breathing inconvenient

COW'S FACE—*GOMUKHASANA*

131

LION·*Simhāsana*

This exercise involves the whole body, but focuses the attention on the mouth and throat.

Sit in a kneeling position with the top of the feet on the floor and the buttocks resting on the heels. Keep the head, neck, and trunk straight. Place the palms of the hands on the knees.

Exhaling, lift the body slightly off the heels and lean forward. In the same movement straighten the arms, keeping the hands on the knees, and spread the fingers apart. Open the mouth as wide as possible and thrust the tongue out and down, trying to touch the chin. Gaze at the point between the two eyebrows. The whole body should feel tensed. Do not inhale while holding this position.

Then inhale, relax, and sit back on the heels.

Benefits:

- Makes the voice soft and melodious

- Aids in relieving a sore throat

- Is said to cure bad breath

LION—*SIMHASANA*

ABDOMINAL LIFT·*Uddiyāna Bandha*

Stand with the feet approximately two feet apart. Keeping the spine straight, bend the knees slightly, and lean forward from the waist only far enough to place the palms of the hands just above the knees.

Exhale completely and place the chin on the hollow of the throat.

Without inhaling, suck the abdominal muscles in and up, pulling the navel toward the spine. This motion pulls the diaphragm up and creates a cavity on the front side of the abdomen under the rib cage.

Hold this position without inhaling as long as it remains comfortable. Then, slowly inhale and relax.

Use force only in pulling the abdominal muscles in, never force the muscles outward.

Do not practice this exercise if you have high blood pressure, hiatal hernia, ulcers, or heart disorders. Women should not practice it during menstruation or pregnancy.

Benefits:
- Promotes health in all the internal organs

- Stimulates digestion

ABDOMINAL LIFT—*UDDIYANA BANDHA*

135

PREPARATION FOR THE HEADSTAND

These two exercises strengthen the muscles of the arms and shoulders.

EXERCISE I

Assume position 8 of the Sun Salutation.

Exhaling, bend the elbows and bring the head as close to the floor as possible between the hands. The nose and chin should not touch the floor and the heels will raise during the movement.

Inhaling, continue to bring the head forward and up. Arch the back so that only the hands and toes remain on the floor.

Return to the original position by pushing the buttocks upward and bringing the head between the arms and hands.

Repeat the exercise three times total.

EXERCISE II

Follow the directions in Step I of the headstand (see page 138). Straighten the legs but do *not* walk the feet toward the body.

Keeping the elbows in the same position place the hands and forearms on the floor parallel to each other and pointing away from the head. Raise the head and look up as high as possible. Hold for three seconds. Interlace the fingers, lower the head and knees and relax.

Repeat three times.

This posture is sometimes referred to as the Dolphin Pose.

HEAD STAND · *Shirshāsana*

STEP 1

Sit in a kneeling position, interlace the fingers and place the hands and forearms on the floor approximately six to nine inches in front of the knees. The elbows should be no further than a forearm's width apart. Raise the hips slightly and place the head (that area approximately two inches in front of the crown of the head) on the floor. The interlaced fingers support the back of the head while the weight of the body remains on the hands and forearms. Therefore, there need be no pressure on the head. Now, straighten the legs, and walk the feet toward the body until the back is perpendicular to the floor.

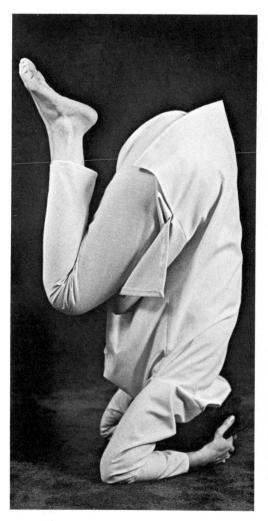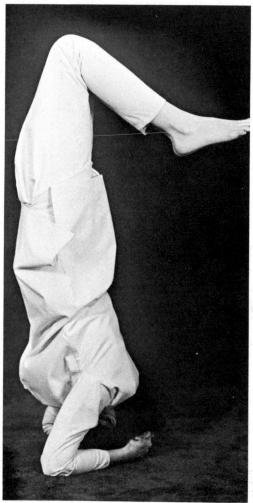

STEP 2

Keeping the back straight, raise both legs, bringing the knees toward the chest and the heels toward the buttocks.

If you find it difficult to raise both legs at the same time and maintain balance, slowly raise one leg while keeping the other on the floor. When this becomes steady, raise the other leg. Do not jerk the legs up suddenly or raise them without complete control. This position is the foundation of the headstand, therefore, it is important that you master it before continuing. Practice this position until you can hold it comfortably for at least 30 seconds before proceeding.

STEP 3

Keeping the heels close to the buttocks, slowly raise the legs until perpendicular to the floor. The knees point toward the ceiling and the lower legs are bent loosely behind the upper legs.

STEP 4

Keeping the body stable, slowly raise the lower legs until the feet point toward the ceiling. Breathe evenly. Hold this position only for as long as is comfortable. Gradually increase the length of time until you can hold this position for one minute.

Concentrate the wieght of the body on the elbows and forearms; there should be very little pressure on the head.

STEP 5

Lower the legs by reversing these steps. Maintain the same control coming out of the headstand as you practiced while entering it.

STEP 6

After returning to the first position, stand up very slowly. Remain standing for as long as you held the posture. This allows the blood flow to return to normal.

STEP 7

Lie in the corpse posture; relax completely.

Steps 6 and 7 are part of the headstand and are as important as the first 5 steps. You may find it convenient to do the headstand last rather than first as the body is already in position for the relaxation exercise in position 7.

Cautions: This is the last posture shown in this manual to be practiced by beginning students. Even young healthy persons should practice the other *asanas* daily for two to three months before attempting the headstand. Persons with the following conditions should not practice this *asana:* high blood pressure, neck problems, weakness in the shoulders, over-weight, or arthritis. Practicing with any of these conditions may cause the vertebrae to actually be **crushed**, resulting in irreversable damage. Do not practice against walls or near furniture or windows.

Benefits:
- Considered the "King of Asanas" in hatha yoga; it is a panacea for all diseases

- Increases the blood pressure and flow of blood to the brain

- Brings exhilaration of spirit and fills the body with energy

- Is said to increase memory and intelligence

HEADSTAND—*SHIRSHASANA*

Relaxation Exercise

After the postures it is beneficial to do a concentrated relaxation exercise. There are many such exercises; the following describes one which relaxes the skeletal muscles, eliminates any fatigue or strain following the postures, and energizes both the mind and the body. During this exercise keep the mind alert and concentrated on your breath as you progressively relax your muscles. Beginners should only practice this exercise for 10 minutes. If practiced longer than 10 minutes the mind usually begins to wander and you may find yourself drifting toward sleep.

TECHNIQUE

Lie in the corpse posture with the eyes gently closed. Inhale and exhale through the nostrils slowly, smoothly, and deeply. There should be no noise, jerks, or pauses in the breath; let the inhalations and exhalations flow naturally without exertion in one continuous movement. Keep the body still.

Mentally travel through the body and relax the top of the head, forehead, eyebrows, space between the eyebrows, eyes, eyelids, cheeks and nose. Exhale and inhale completely four times.

Relax the mouth, jaw, chin, neck, shoulders, upper arms, lower arms, wrists, hands, fingers and fingertips. Feel as if you are exhaling from the fingertips, up the arms, shoulders and face to the nostrils, and inhaling back to the fingertips. Exhale and inhale completely four times.

Relax the fingertips, fingers, hands, wrists, lower arms, upper arms, shoulders, upper back and chest. Concentrate at the center of the chest, and exhale and inhale completely four times.

Relax the stomach, abdomen, lower back, hips, thighs, knees, calves, ankles, feet and toes. Exhale as though your whole body is exhaling, and inhale as though your whole body is inhaling. Expel all your tension, worries and anxieties;

inhale vital energy, peace and relaxation. Exhale and inhale completely four times.

Relax the toes, feet, ankles, calves, thighs, knees, hips, lower back, abdomen, stomach, and chest. Concentrating at the center of the chest exhale and inhale completely four times.

Relax the upper back, shoulders, upper arms, lower arms, wrists, hands, fingers and fingertips. Exhale and inhale completely four times.

Relax the fingertips, fingers, hands, wrists, lower arms, upper arms, shoulders, neck, chin, jaw, mouth, and nostrils. Exhale and inhale completely four times.

Relax the cheeks, eyelids, eyes, eyebrows, space between the eyebrows, forehead and the top of the head. Now, for 30 to 60 seconds, let your mind be aware of the calm and serene flow of the breath . . . let your mind make a gentle, conscious effort to guide your breath so that it remains smooth, calm, and deep, without any noise or jerks.

Slowly and gently open your eyes. Stretch the body. Try to maintain this calm, peaceful feeling throughout the day.

Channel Purification · *Nadi Shodhanam*

PRANAYAMA—CONTROL OF BREATH

Pranayama, the science of breath, follows *asana* as the fourth rung on the ladder of raja yoga as outlined by Patanjali (see page ix of the introduction). The perfection of yoga *asanas* leads one to a natural awareness and deeper understanding of breath and its variations. It is necessary to develop this awareness of breath along with the habit of diaphragmatic breathing before beginning the practice of *pranayama*. Dividing the word *pranayama* clarifies its meaning. *Prana* means life force and *yama* means control, thus, *pranayama* is the control of the life force. *Prana*, or life force refers to the total latent and active energies in man and the universe. This energy in its many manifestations sustains us; it is the vital energy in the sunlight, the food we eat, and the air we breathe. Breath is a vehicle for *prana*, it carries one of the most subtle forms of this vital energy. Therefore, the first and most important step in the practice of *pranayama* is learning to regulate the breath, thereby having control over the motion of the lungs.

ACTIVE AND PASSIVE NOSTRILS

Usually the breath does not flow equally in both nostrils; one nostril is more congested than the other. This can be easily observed; gently close one nostril and inhale and exhale rapidly through the open nostril. Then repeat the same on the opposite side. You will find that one nostril flows more freely than the other; this one is the active nostril, the other is the passive nostril. One inhales *prana* through the active nostril and exhales *prana* through the passive nostril. Throughout the day and night the active and passive nostrils alternate. According to yoga science this phenomenon is the result of the alternating flow of subtle energy in the *ida* and *pingala*, the two main energy channels (*nadis*) along the spinal column. For meditation, it is desirable to activate these two *nadis* equally and apply *sushumna* (state of joy in which both nostrils flow freely).

144

NADI SHODHANAM

There are many methods of *pranayama*, each for a specific purpose. *Nadi shodhanam* is a simple *pranayama* exercise that purifies the *nadis*. It balances the flow of breath in the nostrils and the flow of subtle energy in the *nadis*. *Nadi shodhanam* should be practiced at least twice a day, in the morning and the evening.

(1) Sit in the easy posture with the head, neck, and trunk straight. Inhalation and exhalation should be of equal duration. Do not force the breath; keep it slow, controlled, and free from sounds and jerks. With practice, gradually lengthen the duration of inhalation and exhalation.

(2) Bring the right hand to the nose, fold the index finger and the middle finger so the right thumb can be used to close the right nostril and the ring finger can be used to close the left nostril.

(3) Close the passive nostril and exhale completely through the active nostril.

(4) At the end of exhalation, close the active nostril and inhale through the passive nostril slowly and completely. Inhalation and exhalation should be of equal duration.

(5) Repeat this cycle of exhalation with the active nostril and inhalation with the passive nostril, two more times.

(6) At the end of the third inhalation with the passive nostril, exhale completely through the same nostril keeping the active nostril closed with the finger.

(7) At the end of the exhalation, close the passive nostril and inhale through the active nostril.

(8) Repeat two more times the cycle of exhalation through the passive nostril and inhalation through the active nostril.

(9) To sum up:

1	Exhale	Active
2	Inhale	Passive
3	Exhale	Active
4	Inhale	Passive
5	Exhale	Active
6	Inhale	Passive

7	Exhale	Passive
8	Inhale	Active
9	Exhale	Passive
10	Inhale	Active
11	Exhale	Passive
12	Inhale	Active

(10)   Place the hands on the knees and exhale and inhale through both nostrils evenly for three complete breaths.   This completes ONE cycle of the channel purification exercise.

INDEX

Abdominal breathing, 8
Abdominal Lift, 2, 3, 134-135
Abdominal Muscles, 9, 88, 96
Accomplished Posture, 3
Ahimsa, 6
Angle Posture, 22-25
Aparigraha, 7
Arch Posture, 109
Asana suit, 4
Asanas, ix, x definition; 1, 2, 3, 4, 5, 6,
    42, 43, 59-139
Astanga yoga, ix, 6
Asteya, 6
Auspicious Posture, 3

Back Bending Posture, 68-69
Backaches, 78
Bad Breath, 132
Balance, 2, 96, 126
Balance on Hips, 96-97
Balasana, 122-123
Bhakti Yoga, ix
Bhujangasana, 43, 78-79
Blood Pressure, 2, 106, 134, 140
Boat, 82-83
Boat, half, 80-81
Bow, 88-89
Bow, half, 86-87
Brahmacharya, 6, 7
Breath, 2, 5, 8, 9, 144
Breath Retention, 1, 5
Butterfly, 32-33

Carbon Dioxide, 8, 9
Cat Stretch, 30-31
Chalan, 114-115
Channel Purification, 3, 144-146
Child's Posture, 122-123
Churning, 114-115
Cobra, 3, 78-79
Constipation, 70, 102, 106, 112, 116
Corpse, 3, 66-67
Costal Breathing, 8
Cow's Face, 128-131
Crocodile, 3, 64-65

Dandasana. 43
Dharana, ix, x
Dhyana, ix, x
Dhanurasana, 88-89
Dhanurasana, Ardha, 86-87
Diabetes, 116
Diaphragm, 8, 9, 60, 61

Diaphragmatic Breathing, 8, 9, 60, 61, 64,
    104, 106, 130
Digestion, 106, 112, 116, 134
Dolphin Pose, 137
Double Leg Lifts, 95

Easy Posture, 3, 62
Even Breathing, 1

Fat, 70, 88, 112
Fish, 2, 3
Fish, half, 108

Gas, 78, 91
Gastric Pains, 78
Gomukhasana, 128-131

Ha, x
Halasana, 102-103
Halasana, Ardha, 100-101
Hamstring Muscles, 70, 72
Hand-to-Foot Posture, 70-71
Hatha Yoga, definition, ix, x
Hathayogapradipika, x, 60
Headstand, 2, 136-141
Head-to-Knee, 118-119
Hemorrhoids, 130
Heroic Posture, 128
Hip Joints, 72
Horizontal Stretch, 14-15

Ida, x, 144
Inclined Plane, 120-121
Inverted Action Posture, 104-105
Ishwara Pranidhana, 7

Janushirasana, 118-119
Jnana Yoga, ix
Joints and Glands Exercises, 1

Karma Yoga, ix
"King of Asanas", 140
Knee Joints, 88
Kneeling Posture, 3, 63, 124
Knees-to-Chest Posture, 90
Konasana, 22-25

Lectures on Yoga, 1
Leg Cradles, 34-37
Lion, 63, 132-133
Locust, 85
Locust, half, 84
Lotus Posture, 3, 124

Low Back Pain, 78, 85

Makarasana, 64-65
Mantra, 42
Matsyasana, Ardha, 108
Matsyendrasana, Ardha, 112-113
Meditation, ix, 2, 60, 61, 144
Menstruation, 5, 134
Metabolic Rate, 42

Nadi Shodhana, 3, 144-146
Nadis, 144, 145
Naukasana, 82-83
Naukasana, Ardha, 80-81
Niyamas, ix, 1, 6, 7
Nostrils, 144

Overhead Stretch, 16-17
Oxygen, 9, 42

Padangushthasana, 43
Padhastasana, 43, 70-71
Padmasana, 3
Parathyroid Glands, 106
Paschimottanasana, 116-117
Patanjali, ix, x
Pavanamuktasana, 91
Perineum, 74
Peroneal Nerve, 63
Pingala, x, 144
Plow, 2, 3, 102-103
Plow, Half, 100-101
Posterior Stretch, 116-117
Prana, 144
Pranayama, ix, x, 1, 6, 144, 145
Pratyahara, ix
Pregnancy, 5, 134
Prostate Gland, 118

"Queen of Asanas", 106

Raja Yoga, ix, x
Rectus Abdominis, 8
Relaxation, 2, 3, 5, 64, 66, 126
Relaxation Exercise, 142-143
Respiratory System, 8
Rheumatism, 130
Rocking Chair, 98-99

Samadhi, ix
Samtosha, 7
Shaucha, 7
Sarvangasana, 106-107
Satya, 6
Shalabhasana, 85
Shalabhasana, Ardha, 84
Shavasana, 66-67
Shirshasana, 136-141

Shoulderstand, 2, 3, 106-107
Siddhasana, 3
Side Stretch, 18-19, 72
Simhasana, 132-133
Single Leg Lifts, 92-94
Simple Back Stretch, 20-21
Simple Standing Posture, 12-13
Soorya Namaskara, 42
Sore Throat, 132
Spinal Column, 2, 60, 68, 72, 78, 88,
        102, 112, 116, 144
Spinal Twist, Half, 112-113
Squatting Posture, 126-127
Sukhasana, 3, 62
Sun Salutation, 1, 2, 3, 41-57
Sushumna, 144
Svadhyaya, 7
Swastikasana, 3
Swatmarama, x, 60
Swimming Stretch, 28-29
Symbol of Yoga, 124-125
Symmetrical Stretch, 38-39

Tapas, 7
Textbook of Anatomy &
        Physiology, 8
Tha, x
Thyroid, 106
Torso Twist, 26-27
Tree, 74-77
Triangle, 72-73
Trikonasana, 72-73
Twisting Posture, 110-111

Uddiyana Bandha, 134-135
Ulcers, 134
Urdhvasana, 43, 68-69
Utthita Dwipadasana, 95
Utthita Ekapadasana, 92-94
Utthita Hasta-padasana, 96-97

Vajrasana, 3, 63, 124
Varicose Veins, 104, 106
Veerasana, 128
Venous Blood, 60, 106
Vipritakarani, 104-105
Vrikshasana, 74-77

Wind Eliminating Posture, 91

Yama, 144
Yamas, ix, 1, 6
Yoga, ix, 6
Yoga Mudra, 63, 124-125
Yoga Sutras, ix, x

Zen Posture, 63

HIMALAYAN INSTITUTE PUBLICATIONS

Living with the Himalayan Masters	Swami Rama
Yoga and Psychotherapy	Swami Rama, R. Ballentine, M.D., Swami Ajaya
Emotion to Enlightenment	Swami Rama, Swami Ajaya
A Practical Guide to Holistic Health	Swami Rama
Freedom from the Bondage of Karma	Swami Rama
Book of Wisdom	Swami Rama
Lectures on Yoga	Swami Rama
Life Here and Hereafter	Swami Rama
Marriage, Parenthood and Enlightenment	Swami Rama
Meditation in Christianity	Swami Rama, et al.
Superconscious Meditation	Pandit Usharbudh Arya, Ph.D.
Philosophy of Hatha Yoga	Pandit Usharbudh Arya, Ph.D.
Yoga Psychology	Swami Ajaya
Foundations of Eastern and Western Psychology	Swami Ajaya (ed)
Psychology East and West	Swami Ajaya (ed)
Meditational Therapy	Swami Ajaya (ed)
Diet and Nutrition	Rudolph Ballentine, M.D.
Theory and Practice of Meditation	Rudolph Ballentine, M.D. (ed)
Science of Breath	Rudolph Ballentine, M.D. (ed)
Joints and Glands Exercises	Rudolph Ballentine, M.D. (ed)
Yoga and Christianity	Justin O'Brien, Ph.D.
Inner Paths	Justin O'Brien, Ph.D. (ed)
Faces of Meditation	S. N. Agnihotri, Justin O'Brien, (ed)
Sanskrit Without Tears	S. N. Agnihotri, Ph.D.
Art and Science of Meditation	L. K. Misra, Ph.D. (ed)
Swami Rama of the Himalayas	L. K. Misra, Ph.D. (ed)
Science Studies Yoga	James Funderburk, Ph.D.
Homeopathic Remedies	D. Anderson, M.D., D. Buegel, M.D., D. Chernin, M.D.
Hatha Yoga Manual I	Samskrti and Veda
Hatha Yoga Manual II	Samskrti and Judith Franks
Practical Vedanta	Brandt Dayton
The Swami and Sam	Brandt Dayton
Philosophy of Death and Dying	M. V. Kamath
Chants from Eternity	Institute Staff
Thought for the Day	Institute Staff
Spiritual Diary	Institute Staff
Himalayan Mountain Cookery	Martha Ballentine
The Yoga Way Cookbook	Institute Staff